C000135460

797,885 Books

are available to read at

www.ForgottenBooks.com

Forgotten Books' App
Available for mobile, tablet & eReader

ISBN 978-1-333-83464-7
PIBN 10736713

This book is a reproduction of an important historical work. Forgotten Books uses
state-of-the-art technology to digitally reconstruct the work, preserving the original format
whilst repairing imperfections present in the aged copy. In rare cases, an imperfection in
the original, such as a blemish or missing page, may be replicated in our edition. We do,
however, repair the vast majority of imperfections successfully; any imperfections that
remain are intentionally left to preserve the state of such historical works.

Forgotten Books is a registered trademark of FB &c Ltd.
Copyright © 2017 FB &c Ltd.
FB &c Ltd, Dalton House, 60 Windsor Avenue, London, SW19 2RR.
Company number 08720141. Registered in England and Wales.

For support please visit www.forgottenbooks.com

1 MONTH OF
FREE
READING

at

www.ForgottenBooks.com

By purchasing this book you are eligible for one month membership to ForgottenBooks.com, giving you unlimited access to our entire collection of over 700,000 titles via our web site and mobile apps.

To claim your free month visit:

www.forgottenbooks.com/free736713

* Offer is valid for 45 days from date of purchase. Terms and conditions apply.

English
Français
Deutsche
Italiano
Español
Português

www.forgottenbooks.com

Mythology Photography **Fiction**
Fishing Christianity **Art** Cooking
Essays Buddhism Freemasonry
Medicine **Biology** Music **Ancient**
Egypt Evolution Carpentry Physics
Dance Geology **Mathematics** Fitness
Shakespeare **Folklore** Yoga Marketing
Confidence Immortality Biographies
Poetry **Psychology** Witchcraft
Electronics Chemistry History **Law**
Accounting **Philosophy** Anthropology
Alchemy Drama Quantum Mechanics
Atheism Sexual Health **Ancient History**
Entrepreneurship Languages Sport
Paleontology Needlework Islam
Metaphysics Investment Archaeology
Parenting Statistics Criminology
Motivational

C 6301
U5 L2
opy 1

University and School Extension.

PSYCHOLOGY (Course A).

GEORGE T. LADD,

1889.

Yale University.

Press of J. J. Little & Co.
Astor Place, New York.

HC6301
U5h2

Copyright,
1889,
By GEORGE T. LADD.

[*All rights reserved.*]

COURSE I. DESCRIPTIVE PSYCHOLOGY.*

INTRODUCTORY.

1. **Definition:** What is Psychology? The science may best be defined with reference to its primary *problem*, which is the description and explanation of the states of human consciousness, as such.

[Consider the objections to the customary definition—viz.: " Psychology is the science of the human soul (or mind)"; and compare Ladd's " Elements of Physiological Psychology," p. 1f, and Ward's Article, p. 37.]

---

* This course should be studied topically, following closely the scheme here presented. It is recommended, however, that Sully's " Outlines of Psychology" (D. Appleton & Co., New York : 1884) should be used as a standard of reading and reference, and that each class, or circle, should have for consultation one or more copies of the following works: Bain, " The Senses and the Intellect," and " The Emotions and the Will"; Porter, " Elements of Intellectual Science " ; Dewey, " Psychology"; Janes, " Human Psychology"; Hill, " Elements of Psychology"; Ladd, "Elements of Physiological Psychology"; and Ward, Article on " Psychology," *Encycl. Brit.*, ninth edition. [*N. B.*—Much use should be made of mutual instruction by asking questions of each other and comparing results. Be in no haste to devise set rules for the art of teaching, but strive to attain the greatest amount of mental awakening and growth of power to observe, reflectively, your own mental action and that of others. *Remember that in Psychology the relation of subjects is such that no very clear and complete knowledge of those earliest treated can be obtained until some knowledge of those whose treatment comes later has been reached.*]

2. **Method:** How shall we study Psychology? The true method includes the use of all possible means for acquiring comprehensive, verifiable, and systematized knowledge of the subject: hence the necessity (besides introspection through which the problems of psychology are presented to us) of *observation* (of the phenomena of infant life, savage life, of abnormal states of consciousness, social phenomena, etc.), guided, if possible, by *experiment*, enriched by reflective *reading* (of history, novels, drama, etc., from the psychological point of view), and by study of the opinions of experts. Comparative study of the sentient life of the lower animals is also valuable.

[Criticise the view which regards the immediate observation of one's own mental states (introspection or self-consciousness) as the only method of psychology. Fix the value and relations of each of the foregoing methods.]

3. **Aim:** What should we try to accomplish? The analysis of all the complex states of consciousness into their simplest elements, and the discovery of their laws of combination and sequence; but, especially, the knowledge of the genesis, order, and laws in development of mental life.

[From the points of view now gained, consider the most elementary relations of psychology to education.]

PART FIRST.

MOST GENERAL FORMS OF MENTAL LIFE.

I. **Consciousness** and **Self-consciousness.** The former, as being co-extensive with the existence of any mental fact whatever (the opposite of the "unconsciousness" of the most profound slumber or of a swoon) cannot be defined. The special fact upon which the latter depends is this, that all the states of consciousness are referable, and many of them are actually referred, to a "self." ("I" have the states and know them as *mine*.)

[If self-consciousness be defined as "the (immediate) knowledge which the mind has of its own acts and states," how, and how much can it be used in the study of psychology? Consider, also, the place, limits, and benefits of introspection in education.]

II. **Attention**: Its nature and elementary laws. In what respect, if any, does attention differ from the varying amount of psychical activity as directed toward any particular object of consciousness?

[Sully: chap. iv.; and Ward's Art., p. 41f.]
[Consider the training of attention as necessary to education.]

III. **Knowledge, Feeling, Will** :—the so-called "Faculties" of the mind, and the differences of the phenomena on which the distinction of faculties depends. Are there distinguishable and irreducible modes of the behavior of mind (or classes of the states of consciousness) ; and, if so, what and how many are these modes? How is their existence consistent with the unity of mind?

[Consider the relation of these so-called "faculties," and their interdependence in education.]

PART SECOND.

ELEMENTS OF MENTAL LIFE.

I. **Sensation** : Psychological science recognizes an elementary and necessary, but theoretical, factor of our sense-experience, called the "simple" sensation. (In organized, self-conscious experience, there are no simple or isolated sensations.)

1. **The Nature of Sensation**: its necessary pre-conditions in physical stimulus (light- and sound waves, heat, etc.) and physiological action ("nerve-commotion" in the end-organs—such as the eye, ear, skin, etc.,—in the nerve-tracts, and central organs, of the nervous system).

[N. B.—*The sensation itself is always and purely a psychical state* (or event) due to the characteristic reaction of the mind, when certain physiological processes take place as conditions.]

2. **Quality** (what sort ?) **of Sensation.**

[Consider its great variety under each one of the principal senses : *e. g.* shades of color, pitch of tones, kinds of smells, etc.]

3. **Quantity** (how much ?) **of Sensation.** On what do the varying degrees of quantity depend, and what is the relation between them and the changes in the amount of the physical stimulus ?

[Weber's law :—See Sully, p. 114f, and Ladd, p. 365f.]

4. Local Coloring of Sensation.

[On this subject compare with Sully the statement in Lotze's "Outlines of Psychology," p. 51f, on the existence and nature of "local signs."]

5. **The Kinds of Senses.** Besides the *five senses* customarily distinguished, may we not enumerate, sixth, the *muscular sense* (on the "muscular feelings," see Bain, vol. I., pp. 74–100) ; seventh, the *sense of temperature ;* and eighth, vague general sense (*sensus communis*)?

II. **Ideation.** The simplest mental state corresponding to this term would be one marked by the occurrence of an image representative of a single sensation previously experienced. But here, as in the case of the sensation itself, we find in organized experience no perfectly simple or isolated representative images ; indeed, the very term "representation" implies a reference to a somewhat complex and developed mental life.

1. **Conditions of Ideation :** (*a*) physical, as shown in the phenomena of "after-images," etc., and implied in the laws of habit ; (*b*) mental, particularly attention, interest, etc.

[Consider the analogies of physical registration and reproduction of impressions outside of the body.]

2. **Nature of the Representative Image** (or "idea"):—This determined as respects its strength, clearness, completeness (or fullness of content), and relations of similarity or dissimilarity to the original from which it is derived.

[In what sense can such an image be said to be *like* or *unlike* a sensation ?]

3. **Kinds of Representative Images** (or "ideas"):
(*a*) The memory image, or "idea" representative of some previous individual impression. (*b*) The image of phantasy, or the "idea" severed from all connections of time and place pertaining to the original impressions.

III. **Feeling.**

[Consider whether, strictly speaking, *feeling*, as such, can be described or treated scientifically, since description and science are forms of cognition only.]

1. **Nature of Feeling**: its pure subjectivity, incommunicable character, and its relation to knowledge.

[Must we know in order to feel, or is not feeling, the rather, as primitive a form of psychical activity as either sensation or ideation?]

2. **The Tone of all Feeling,**—is either *pleasure* or *pain*.
What tone characterizes each particular feeling depends upon several considerations, such as the condition of the organism when stimulated, the strength of the stimulus, habit, fixation or wandering of attention, the relation to each other of the different elements in the "field of consciousness," etc.

[Are there strictly neutral or indifferent feelings?]

3. **Kinds of Feeling**:

(*a*) Sensuous feelings, or those which accompany the action of the organs of sense and fuse with the different resulting sensations. (*b*) Intellectual feelings, or those which accompany the processes of ideation and thought.

[Consider whether the feelings, as such, can be classified, or are indefinite in number and variety, so that all classification has regard to the kinds of bodily and mental activities in conjunction with which feeling arises, and with which it "fuses," as it were, rather than to the feeling, as such.]

Feelings may also be either (*a*) simple or (*b*) composite (or mixed).

[Reserve the consideration of the higher composite and intellectual feelings and their development, until Part Third, Section IV., is reached.]

IV. **Desire.** Under this head fall the half-blind (but only *half-*blind) appetites, instincts, and impulses, as well as the more clearly conscious mental states of attraction and repulsion toward an object.

[Consider whether desire can be regarded—in the customary way—as a mere form of feeling. Is it not rather a new form of psychical activity, dependent, indeed, upon a peculiar combination of an experience of pleasurable and painful feeling with an activity of ideation?]

V. **Volition.**

[*N. B*—For the present all consideration of questions of freedom of choice (or of the will) should be refused, and attention concentrated upon the psychological origin and nature of those peculiar states of consciousness which depend upon the mental representation of an idea of action accompanied by the desire to realize the idea, and which are characterized by that special kind of spontaneity which causes them to be called " acts of will."]

Volition, or " acts of will," need to be distinguished, with especial care, from desires and impulses, the most nearly allied forms of psychical activity.

1. **Conditions of Volition :** (*a*) Physical,—a sensory-motor mechanism capable of reflex and so-called " automatic " (or spontaneous) action, stimulation of this mechanism, etc.; (*b*) mental.

[Here consider the relations of feeling, desire, ideation, and, especially, attention, to the forthputting of volition (" act of will ").]

.2. **Kinds of Volition.** These are determined by the relation in which the act of will stands to the previous states of consciousness, or to the elements of the same mental state of which it is a part. (*a*) Forced volitions, or undeliberated and "uni-motived" acts of will.

[Consider whether this involves any contradiction of terms: *e. g.*, an act of attention may be held to involve an act of will, but it is certainly not always "voluntary" in the sense of involving choice.]

(*b*) Voluntary " acts of will " (or choices).

[Under this topic of "volition" falls the consideration of the dependence of the bodily movements—sensory-motor, ideo-motor, etc.—upon the states of consciousness.]

VI. **Primary Intellection** (Discrimination and Judgment). *Discrimination* is the necessary condition of all knowledge, whether of self or of things, and of all growth of mental life. Without it there could be no self-recognition or distinction of " kinds of mental states," whether of sensation, ideation, or feeling.

1. **Nature of Judgment :**—this involves a *relating* activity of mind, which may be regarded as a secondary and higher form of reaction in it, stimulated by its own states of sensation and ideation. (*a*) Relation of judgment to sensation and ideation (dependence on these activities). (*b*) Relation of judgment to belief and doubt, in their most primitive forms. (*c*) Relation of the two factors (as indicated by subject and predicate) in every judgment (*e. g.* affirmative or negative).

2. **Qualities of Judgment;**—such as clearness, accuracy, promptness, etc.

3. **Kinds of Judgment:** (*a*) Psychological or primary judgment (the discrimination of mental states and positing— as it were—in consciousness of the result). (*b*) Judgment of reality (the affirmation or negation of a quality or relation as belonging to a real being). (*c*) Logical judgment (the relating, affirmatively or negatively, of general notions).

[N. B.—The two latter kinds of judgment involve a complex development of the mental powers,—cognition of " Things" as objectively existing and formation of general notions by processes of thought; but their essence is to be found in the same discerning and relating activity of the mind.] .

PART THIRD.

THE DEVELOPMENT OF MENTAL LIFE.

I. **The Acquisition of Perceptions** (or so-called " Presentations of Sense ").

[Consider that to perceive " Things" is a mental achievement which belongs, in its most essential respects, to our earliest life; and the processes of which, therefore, cannot be recalled or pictured in forms of our present organized experience. And " Things" themselves are not existences ready-made, independently of the activity of mind, and then, in some mysterious way, carried over into and impressed upon the mind. The Mind, according to its own laws, constructs the perceptions of sense.]

1. **Conditions of Perception:** These are to be found in the character and relations of the different classes of

sensations and images of sensations,—especially those of sight and touch ; and in the activity of mind in—so to speak —dealing with these sensations and images. *Judgment, also, is involved in all activity of the mind in perception.*

2. **Stages of Perception**: (*a*) Discrimination and combination ("mental synthesis") of sensations. (*b*) Localization of sensations. (*c*) Association, with present sensations, of images of previous sensations, whether of the same or of different senses. (*d*) Perception of our own body and of "Things" as distinguished from each other. (*e*) So-called "acquired perceptions" (strictly speaking, all perceptions are acquired), by means of secondary signs and more complex processes of reasoning.

[Here refer to Part Second, I., 4, and reconsider the theory of "local signs."] [See Ladd, p. 443f.]

3. **Special Channels of Perception**: (*a*) Tactual perception. (*b*) Visual perception.

[Consider, in particular, the construction of the space-qualities and space-relations of things, by the activity of these two senses.]

4. **Illusions of Perception.**

[These should be studied chiefly for the light they throw upon the nature of the perceptive process itself. Remember that, in every case of so-called "errors of sense," the mind acts with precisely the same powers and under the same laws as those which characterize its so-called "normal" action.]

5. **Theories of Perception.**

[See Porter, p. 189f, and Janes, p. 126f.]

II. **The Formation of Memory and Imagination** (or the Growth of Representative Knowledge).

1. **Conditions of Representative Knowledge:**
(*a*) The limitations of consciousness: these narrow the field of ideation, and prevent the distribution of attention—so to speak—over an indefinite number of objects. (*b*) The unity of consciousness: this compels all the ideas, when recurring in consciousness, to observe certain relations of fusion, or of recognized similarity, or recognized difference.

2. **Laws of the Reproduction of Ideas:** (*a*) Fusion of the ideas. The different simpler ideas (or, rather, states of ideation), on combining to produce the more complex, act and react on each other, according to their mutual relations, whether of agreement, or inhibition, etc. (*b*) Immediate or direct reproduction of ideas. Different previous states of ideation tend—with more or less strength as dependent on temperament, mood, accompaniment of feeling, degree of attention originally given to them, etc.—to recur spontaneously. (*c*) Mediate or indirect reproduction of ideas (the "Association of ideas"). Existing states of ideation are explicable by immediately previous states (the previous states being said to "induce," or "suggest" the existing states); and all existing states of ideation tend to produce certain following states rather than others (the latter being dependent on the mental "tendencies" expressed in the former).

The different forms of "Association" are customarily declared to be : (1) association by contiguity ; (2) association by similarity ; (3) association by contrast.

[Consider that "contiguity," as here used, means *mental* contiguity (co-existence or close sequence of the elementary or more complex phases of mental life); and, then, examine what is the reason for this alleged power of contiguity, and whether similarity and contrast, apart from contiguity, have other than an indirect influence.]

3. Kinds of Representative Knowledge :

(*A*) *Memory*,—considered as involving (1) recognition ; and (2) the mental representation of time ; (3) the formation of memory.

[Note carefully the difference between having a succession of ideas and having, even the most elementary, idea of succession.]

(*B*) *Imagination*,—either as (1) mainly reproductive in the lower forms of activity (e. g., reveries, dreaming, etc.); or, as (2) mainly constructive (in the discovery of scientific and philosophical truth, the invention of practical contrivances, and in art).

[Consider the laws of reproductive and constructive ideation as related to the cultivation of memory and imagination, and to education generally.]

III. **Thought (proper) and the Attainment of Scientific Knowledge.** By that secondary and higher reaction of the Mind on the elements of experience (combined and associated sensations and representative images), which we call "Thinking," new combinations are formed and are regarded as necessary (independent of sense-impressions and of the laws of the association of ideas) and universal.

1. **Nature of Thought.** All *thought* (properly so-called) is the mental affirmation or negation of a relation between the particular and the universal.

[Compare Part Second, VI., 1 and 3.]

2. **Stages and Products of Thought.** (*A*) *Concepts* (or general notions): (1) their nature, as related to the images of memory and phantasy ; (2) their formation, as dependent on primary judgment, abstraction, generalization, naming, etc. (compare Part Second, VI.); (3) their extent and content ; (4) their perfection and imperfection.

(*B*) *Judgments* (of the secondary sort, as involving the formation and relating of general notions): (1) their elements, as indicated by the words "subject," "predicate," "copula"; (2) their kinds (analytic and synthetic ; judgments of extent and of content).

(*C*) *Reasoning*,—as involving the relating, the concatenating or linking-together, of judgments. (1) The kinds of reasoning (inductive and deductive ; the forms of the syllogism, etc.). (2) Degrees of conviction produced by reasoning (certainty, probability, etc.).

3. **The Construction of Science.**

[In what respects does "scientific knowledge differ from ordinary knowledge ; and are these points of difference, psychologically considered, essential ?]

(*a*) The experimental and other tests of science. (*b*) Scientific systemization. (*c*) The induction of laws.

4. Relations of Thought and Language.

5. Universal and Necessary Forms of Thought.

[Here consider the origin and nature of such ideas as those of *Being, Reality,* and, especially, *Cause;* also *Final Purpose.*]

[Consider all the foregoing facts and laws as related to the training of the judgment and reasoning powers; also, the relation of culture in thought to education.]

IV. The Formation of the Emotions and Sentiments.

Both emotions and sentiments involve a somewhat complexly organized experience of perception, ideation, and thought,— the sentiments, however, more clearly than the emotions.

(*A*) *The Emotions:* these develop earlier than the sentiments, and are characterized by a greater strength of the attack—so to speak—which they make upon the ideating activities; and by the greater prominence of the bodily basis upon which they rest (characterized by physical agitation).

(*B*) *The Sentiments:* (*a*) Intellectual; (*b*) Æsthetic; (*c*) Ethical.

[Consult, especially, the excellent remarks of Sully, pp. 480–568. Consider the possibility and means of cultivating the emotions and sentiments, and the relations of such culture to general education.]

V. The Development of Will (Choice, Conduct, Character).

[Consider again the distinction between such spontaneous motor activity as is accompanied by the feeling of effort and by the direction of attention, and deliberate choice. See Part Second, V., 1 and 2.]

1. **Factors Necessary to Choice.** (*a*) Mental representation of two or more ends to be gained and of the means necessary to their attainment. (*b*) Excitement of the sensibility in the form of desire. (*c*) Deliberation, or conflict of so-called "motives" regulated by the direction of attention. (*d*) Decision,—the appropriation to self of one end, and its system of means, to the exclusion of others (*choice*, peculiarly so designated). (*e*) Fiat of will (accompanied by the "feeling of effort," and resulting, under physical and psychical laws, in starting the train of means deemed necessary to the attainment of the chosen end).

[These factors may, of course, be so compressed, or nearly fused, as it were, that their accomplishment shall include only a brief time.]

2. **Conditions of the Development of Will.** (*a*) Control of the bodily organism and of the train of ideas, involving the voluntary fixation of attention. (*b*) Formation of complex ideas and sentiments (especially the ethical). (*c*) Formation of habits of choice.

3. **Conduct and the Formation of Character.**

(*A*) *Conduct*,—which, as distinguished from mere physical and psychical activity, involves the development of complex and organized experience (sentiments, ideas, thought, and "choices" as distinguished from the mere forthputting of volitions).

LIBRARY OF CONGRESS

0 029 944 919 1

(*B*) *Character.* (*a*) Definition of character. (*b*) Elements of character. (*c*) Dependence of character on ideals. (*d*) Relation of the law of habit to character.

[Consider now the laws and means of the training of Will, and the relation of all education to the forming of character.]

VI. History and General Laws of Mental Development.

1. **Meaning of Mental Development** (the life of the soul advancing to the realization of its idea).

2. **Principles of Mental Development.** (*a*) Combination of internal and external influences, and reaction of a psychical nature upon environment, as involved in all development. (*b*) Interdependence of body and mind, and of all the so-called "faculties." (*c*) Order in the organization of experience. (*d*) Variety of individuals and mental unity of the race.

3. **Stages of Mental Development.**

[Here read, if possible, Preyer's "The Mind of the Child" (Part I., by D. Appleton & Co., New York, 1888), and consider its bearing upon the whole problem of the order, method, and amount of study and teaching required for the best education of the young.]

4. **The Final Purpose of Mental Development.** How shall this be defined?

CPSIA information can be obtained
at www.ICGtesting.com
Printed in the USA
BVHW041048170119
538075BV00017B/1096/P

9 781333 834647